Event Planning: Management & Marketing For Successful Events

by Alex Genadinik

ISBN: 1519178204
ISBN-13: 978-1519178206

DEDICATION

Dedicated to my mother and grandmother who are the biggest entrepreneurs I know.

CONTENTS

FOREWORD

The advice in this book is based on my experience of creating a successful event series from scratch. My hope is that sharing what I learned from creating my own event series will help you find success with your events and your greater business. Enjoy the book, and feel welcome to get in touch with me if you have further questions or face business challenges beyond the scope of this book.

BEFORE WE START

Hello, I am excited that you got this book, and I want to extend a very warm welcome to you. In writing this book I did my best to cover every element that I think will make your events a success.

The book is based on my own experience creating a successful event series from scratch. Throughout the book (especially in the second chapter which covers marketing), there are real life examples of what happened to me when I was building my own event series, how I overcame challenges, and eventually found success. This way you have a practical case study to give you additional perspectives in addition to event theory.

GIFTS FOR YOU

In an effort to make sure that you truly get a lot of value from this book, I added 3 additional free resources at the end of this book. Browse all the resources there, and definitely take advantage of the extra freebies.

CHAPTER 1: EVENT MANAGEMENT & FUNDAMENTALS OF RUNNING A SUCCESSFUL EVENT SERIES

"Whether you think you can, or you think you can't, you are right."

- Henry Ford

1. My story and case study of how I created a successful event series

How do I know about starting a successful event series? Well, years ago I naively started a business which was essentially a group hiking website. Every hike was essentially an event that required its own organizing, planning, marketing and a way to generate sufficient revenue. We'll touch on all of this as we make our way through the book.

My hiking business turned out to be my first reasonably successful business, but how I got it to be a success was very far from a straight line. It was an incredible struggle before I saw any sign of success.

If you are curious to take a look at what the business once was, even though I don't currently run this business, the website is still up at:
http://www.comehike.com so that you can get a sense for what the business was.

As you can see from the website, it was quite an amateur effort. But despite the website being amateure, despite my lack of experience at the time, and despite the many beginner beginner mistakes I had made along the way, I was able to make the event part of the business a big success. Later in this book I'll get into details of how the business became a success.

But first, let me explain to you the mistaken initial business strategy I had for this business, and what I later identified as my biggest errors. I hope that seeing my mistakes might help you avoid making similar errors yourself.

I thought that people hate event websites like meetup.com because the organizers have to pay a monthly fee. So I thought I would make money by keeping my site free, and by publishing ads on my website. In my mind this was a winning strategy because it give event organizers a free option to manage their hikes or other outdoor events, and for that reason they would flock to my website and abandon meetup.

My main mistakes (there were many smaller ones not worth mentioning yet):

1) The ad revenue model only works for websites with a LOT of traffic because on average my Google ads (AdSense ads) made $6 per every 1,000 page views.

   This means that even if I got 100,000 monthly page views, I would only be making $600 which isn't even enough to pay half of my rent. And to make a decent American middle class salary of $6,000/month I would need 1,000,000 page views each month which is very difficult to do for such a small niche website. So the monetization strategy was too weak for the kind of business that this was. I was pursuing a losing strategy from day one!

2) My second mistake was competing with a thriving, loved and growing website like meetup.com because it proved very difficult to get hike organizers to switch to my website from Meetup because Meetup had so much more quality and tens of thousands of hikers, which my website obviously did not. Plus, as you probably experienced for yourself, when you first came to my website, you saw that it was an amateur effort while Meetup is a nicely made professional website.

3) Poor website design and branding which you can immediately see by visiting comehike.com - this hurt the growth of my business in a big way.

As you can see, from day one, my business was a losing effort. But I didn't quit. I figured out how to keep my head above water, and did it precisely by making the outdoor events that I put on into epic ones that got the whole zity buzzing.

My hope is that by the end of this book you will have the knowledge and the ideas to apply what I did with my events to yours, and make your event series a tremendous success.

And let me leave you with a thought to ponder as we get close to the end of the opening section of this book. Since I made so many large obvious mistakes, the one thought that haunted me for years after having started this business was that if I had a mentor or a good advisor, in literally 5 minutes of conversation they could have steered me away from most of my mistakes, and that would have saved me money and many months of struggle. And if you get a good mentor, that might help you tremendously as well.

But that struggle that I had to go through to "wiggle out" of my mistakes was what allowed me to create a great outdoor event series that went from a total disaster to being talked about on NPR (National Public Radio), generating a significant amount of money, getting me a lot of publicity, and ultimately making this business successful.

As this book moves forward, especially in the second chapter on marketing, I will also share what happened in my own event series at different times, so that you will see the case study of my own experience and hopefully will be able to apply it to your events to avoid big mistakes on your the path to success.

2. The basics of creating a successful event series and what you need to keep in mind

The biggest thing that will help you is consistency over the long term. People almost never get it right from their very first event (or even in the first few months as it was in my case). There are many things that have to fall into place like marketing, event quality, and many other factors. It simply takes time to get all the details right.

I had to go through significant struggle before my events took off and grew, and I want to encourage you not to give up as well. Struggle is a part of your journey to success. Trust me, I fully realize how frustrating it is to go through struggle. I've been there myself. I know how you feel. But you must-must-must push through those moments.

My own event series, when it first started, would get zero or just a handful of attendees. It was a frustrating and depressing experience for me. But If I had used that as a sign to stop, I would have never found the success much later.

So even before you start your first event, try to focus on the long-term, and position the event series as a long-term project. That way you will refine the problems over time, and after lots of trial and error you will get it right, and find success. But it will only come from *consistency*. Over time you will turn your weaknesses into strengths, and become successful.

Personally, when I was struggling, I used to hate it when people used to tell me that one day I will be successful. But then one day, if you are consistent and work hard over time, you will become successful too. Eventually it just happens, and it will happen to you too. Just make sure to work hard over time. That's really the difference maker, and why I am emphasizing this point so much here.

So if you don't get great results at first, don't be discouraged. Initial failure is common. Just keep hacking away at it.

Another common thing you must figure out for your event series is the balance of price vs. growth. Obviously if you make events free, you will attract maximum attendance, but as soon as you start charging even as low as $1 you will immediately and significantly decrease attendance. You always have to balance between growing attendance as aggressively as possible and. making money from the events. I will cover how to manage this later in the book so that you can have the most rapid growth while making the most amount of money.

Here is my **3-part formula for having a successful event series**, and almost any other business. It is like a 3-legged stool where all 3 legs have to work. If one leg doesn't work, the stool falls, and in case of the event series, it doesn't succeed. So the three "legs" are:

1) Marketing and growth
2) Event quality
3) It has to make sense financially, and generate enough revenue to meet your financial goals for the events

Always have these most important aspects in mind when thinking about your event series, and try to align these 3 aspects of your overall strategy to work well together.

3. Ways in which you can generate revenue from your events

The most obvious way to generate revenue is to charge individuals for attending the events. And there is a right time to do that. But as already noted, charging for events will reduce attendance growth. So let's explore some ways you can generate revenue by keeping your events free.

One common thing you can try to do is to have sponsors. Sponsors come in a few shapes and sizes. You can have sponsors who will directly give you cash to promote something of theirs, provide a venue for your events, or provide something free to give away during your events in a contest or a raffle drawing.

Of course, since we are now focusing on generating revenue, we care about sponsors that contribute cash. Keep in mind that sponsors typically want to reach a significant number of people. So the sooner you build a big list of attendees and get their email addresses, or regularly have very high attendance, the sooner sponsors will flock to your events. But keep in mind that trying to get sponsors too early might be a waste of time because if you don't have many people to promote the events to, sponsors won't be too interested.

Over time, if you do noteworthy things and get some publicity, sponsors will begin reaching out to you. But that is only over time, if you are *consistent* and eventually successful.

When I ran my own event series, of course, I made the mistake of trying to get sponsors too early. All that resulted in was some conversations that eventually resulted in a NO, and wasted my time. But as my events grew, I was able to have more fruitful and successful conversations with different sponsors and partners for my events. Once different companies saw that I was able to get their products in front of many people who fit their ideal customer profiles, they were all too eager to send me free samples of their products (which you can keep or use as raffle prizes) or cash in exchange for promotion.

Another way you can generate revenue at your events is by selling food or products. This is especially good if you have a longer event because people will get hungry, and you can sell them food directly, or get a vendor to pay you to be present at your event and sell food there.

In my case, since I ran outdoor events, I would come to my hiking events with a car full of things like sunscreen, hats, water and light snacks, and just let people know that these are available for purchase if they forgot it at home. And, of course, many people did forget those items at home, and ended up buying them from me.

It wasn't a lot of money and truthfully, there was some awkwardness in announcing that I have things for sale right at the beginning of the event before the attendees got any value from the event, but at times when I did this, it put an extra bit of revenue directly in my pocket, which was certainly welcome, and it didn't hurt attendance.

Once you have sponsors, it is also a great way to give them a plug by giving away something free of theirs at the beginning of the event that the attendees might find useful and appreciate. Just a word of warning: don't give away any old thing. Make sure that it actually does make the lives of your attendees better.

Another very interesting thing you can try to do to generate revenue from free events is to ask for donations, or ask people to pay whatever price they choose. What that does is it allows you to keep your events listed as free and to generate maximum attendance. At the same time, if people enjoy the event, and you ask for donations in a professional, polite but assertive way, you will be surprised by how many people will give you donations.

You might also be pleasantly surprised by the size of a few of those donations which might be higher than what you expected. But that would happen only if the people truly loved and enjoyed your events. So don't forget about that leg of the 3-legged stool which is your event quality.

Keep in mind that not everyone will donate or pay if given a choice. But because you maximized attendance by making it free, giving people the option to donate and to choose the amount will balance out the people who come for free.

Using this strategy, you can get a surprisingly similar number of attendees who give you donations as you would if you just charged for attendance upfront, but limited the total number of attendees.

Another way to make money from your events is to sell them branded products like t-shirts, hats or anything that will be useful to them, and have your logo and maybe website (that could be a bit too much) printed on those products. This way you can generate extra revenue while turning people into, as I endearingly call them, walking advertisements for your business.

And by the way, you yourself should be a walking advertisement for your business by having a branded shirt and maybe even a hat during your events. I'll touch more on this in a later section of the book.

If your events take only a few hours, and not more than a full day, what you can do is up-sell longer, maybe full-weekend seminars or getaways for which you can charge hundreds or even thousands of dollars per person. This isn't easy to do when you start, but once you've grown a bit, and people recognize and trust your brand, or you have some loyal attendees who attend regularly, you can pitch the bigger full-day or multi-day events to your most loyal and engaged attendees because in those longer events they would ideally get much more value and enjoyment.

Another strategy you can employ to generate revenue from your events is to up-sell some of your professional or consulting services, or some high-end products of yours if you have a business that sells any products or services.

Another thing some people do is use an event series to make themselves "an authority" in their business niche. Having a big event series of which you are the organizer makes you a visible and popular person in your industry. As a result of that, many people will want to work with you and network with you because you have a significant asset (your events) that you own, out of which can come multiple benefits for people.

Being such an authority or "mover and shaker" in your industry or business niche can get you jobs or consulting contracts that will pay you much more than you would typically get paid at similar jobs if you didn't have your event series.

And very often in the cases of such jobs or consulting projects, they only become available to you as a result of having a big event series and a large marketing reach. So you can make pretty significant money from your events in an indirect way like this.

There are many indirect benefits for becoming an authority or a known person/brand in your industry. People will begin to want to be associated with you and want to network with you. That will result in more publicity for you and your business, more favors for you and your business, and that publicity and favors is something I will touch more on in later sections of the book, especially when discussing marketing and promotion for your events.

In the case of my own event series, once I started generating publicity for my events (and I will teach you how to do that for your events shortly), those publicity pieces came in the form of articles which linked to my website. And that helped my SEO (search engine optimization) which propelled my website up in Google search rankings and drove much more attendance to my business. So look forward to my tips on how to do that, a little later in this book when I discuss the marketing for your events.

Also, something to really keep and mind and something that I will also cover in the section on marketing your events is the idea of identifying people who are willing to pay and spend money, and getting them to spend money again and again. Every business or event series has a top 5% or 10% of people who come in contact with it, and love that business so much that they become regular customers and spend a disproportionate amount more money than everyone else.

You must identify who those people are, treat them extra well, and offer additional products specifically to them or with them in mind. These are the types of people who might be interested in your multi-day events whereas other people who casually attend won't really be ready to buy premium products.

And before I move on, let me list a couple of additional benefits of making your events free. First, if there is another event series out there with similar events to yours, and they charge money to attend, you can suffocate their attendance by making yours free, and drawing many of their attendees to leave their events and attend yours.

Another benefit of having a free event is that you can get the free attendees who appreciate that your events are free to promote your events on their social media accounts, and to invite their friends. This will give you an even faster rate of growth for your event series. And ironically, if people bring friends, due to peer pressure and not wanting to seem like a jerk in front of their friends, they will give more and bigger donations when you ask for those donations (or ask people to choose whatever price they want to pay for the event).

This is actually what happened in my events. Whenever I asked people to donate, consistently the biggest donors were couples. The guys used to give bigger than average donations because they felt the scrutiny and pressure by their dates, and didn't want to appear cheap.

4. How to choose a price for your events if you do charge for attendance

As you just read, there are many options for you to make money from events without having to charge for attendance directly. But there may be a point when you are ready to set a price for your event. So let's cover how to choose the ideal price for your event series.

In general pricing theory, it is widely agreed that going up in price is easier than going down. What that means for you is that starting at a relatively low price points is a fine thing to do because you can go up in price from there. And gradually going up in price lets you test how many people attend at different price points so that over time you can identify an ideal price point which generates maximum revenue for your events.

Plus, having a cheaper price gives you an extra marketing weapon/angle because you can tell people that your future events will be more expensive and they "should take advantage of current low prices."

Does that phrase sound familiar? Using low price discounts and promotions is a widely used tactic in advertisements and promotions. You hear this in just about every commercial break on TV, especially in car commercials where they throw in phrases like "while supplies last" which creates a feeling of scarcity and gets people to rush to buy the product! So if creating scarcity works for those other businesses, it can work for you if you tell people that this low price offer is only available for a limited time, and only for this event (or some time period) and will go up soon.

Long-term, whatever prices you choose, you can entice people to attend by offering them discounts. What discounts do is kind of shock people with a high price, and then give them a lower price. After the shock of the higher price, the lower price seems much better. Plus, it lets you raise prices while still allowing to keep the price low for some people.

You can also use discounts to create urgency. For example, if the event is one month away, you can give a 50% discount to people who buy tickets a month in advance, and only a 25% discount to people who buy 1 week in advance and a 10% discount to people who buy 3 days in advance. People will jump on the cheaper discounted offer and start swelling your attendance number.

For most events, a majority of people decide on whether they will attend in the last few days. And if they see that the event already has so many registrants a month or a week in advance, it will make it appear as though the event is even more special and unique than what they thought it would be, and that would get people to decide to come at the last minute, and pay premium prices.

As your events grow and you start to have trouble meeting demand and selling the events out, that will be a good time to begin either raising prices or getting a larger venue. The more you raise prices, the more you decrease attendance. But the quality of each attendee who pays a higher price is higher.

Since they are willing to pay higher prices, the attendees will have more natural interest in the content of the events, and will be more likely to spend money on other things you try to sell to them. So raising prices (while providing great value) is a great way to reach higher-end clients.

Many businesses really covet higher end clients because those people can spend more money. But I want to give you some food for thought on that point. Walmart is more profitable than any high end designer brand. If you can get many people to pay a lower price and just get a bigger space for your event, it might be more lucrative than having fewer high-end clients pay higher prices.

But take all that with a grain of salt. Since there are so many kinds of events out there, I can't know what price or client discount strategy would work best for your unique situation. What you must do is experiment and calibrate. Also, talk to your event attendees, and get their thoughts on the pricing, and other aspects of your events. Especially ask them how to improve your events. They will surely have many opinions how you can do better. You don't necessarily have to take all of their advice, especially since the advice will often be directly conflicting, but you can always give it some thought, and use it to inform whatever decisions you will make in the future.

Quick note on charging for events or charging for anything else: many first-time entrepreneurs have a hard time charging for something. I am not saying that this is necessarily the case for you, but it is likely that if this is your first business, you may feel some apprehension about charging for events. I know that this was the case for me when I started. Asking people for money can be awkward. And I probably maximized the awkwardness of it because I recall feeling very uneasy about charging people money.

I would advise to take that leap and charge at least a small fee. If you are really apprehensive about charging, maybe keep the events free until you are certain that people are getting great value from the events. That knowledge will make you more confident when charging.

Plus, your efforts and your time are worth you getting paid. And if your attendees see your low confidence in your pricing strategy, they will read into it that the event really isn't worth the price. After all, if even the event organizer doesn't appear confident in their pricing or asking people to pay, how can the attendees be expected to feel good about paying? So try to be confident about your event quality and about your time being worth getting paid for.

5. Hiring staff for your event

If your event series grows to be big enough, you will need to hire some staff. So let me explain how to get staff for free or at a very affordable rate.

As soon as you start charging for attendance, you will get some people asking you for a favor to give them free access. These people will probably never pay anyway. So what you can do is give them free access in exchange for doing some job at the event. This is a simple way to get some free labor and make some friends because those people will most likely appreciate that you gave them free entrance to your paid event.

If you can't get enough free labor, you can get very cheap (or is the politically correct term "affordable" labor?) on local concierge websites. A couple of such popular websites are fancyhands.com and taskrabbit.com - there you can find people who will do odd jobs, and you can hire them for a day to help out with your event.

Just a quick note on these kinds of sites, in different countries and cities, different such sites are popular. So wherever you live, the website examples I gave may or may not be the most popular sites. What I recommend that you do is first check out those websites, but if you don't find any great help there, just search Google for something like "hire someone for one day in your_city_name" where your_city_name is the name of your actual city. Or try a variety of similar searches until you find a good website for this sort of thing for your local area.

In United States, for a full day's work, these people will often charge only $100 or possibly less. So you get good value from them. And for just a few hours worth of work you can maybe get away with paying under $50 or even $30.

If you charge for events, and these laborers will help to improve the quality of the event, and help you make the event run more smoothly, it will help to get more people to enjoy the events, and to recommend your future events to their friends, and themselves attend more of your events.

Additionally, the more people enjoy your events, the more likely they will be to engage with whatever products or services you try to sell them. So hiring help can seem like a waste of money, but if the people you hire help to make the events better, it can help to generate revenue for you to more than compensate for the help you hired.

Another way to get free labor at your events is to ask friends and family to help out. Not everyone will be excited to help you, but some friends and family might actually be eager to help you and to see you succeed. So a few people might jump at the opportunity to help you. It will be a nice way to do something together with them while getting free labor for your events.

One caveat, of course, is that it is often risky to mix friends, family and business. Some disagreements may lead to harming your relationships with your friends and family. So you should think twice before inviting your friends and family to help at your events because you certainly don't want to risk harming the relationships you have with them.

Another point on growing your events and hiring staff is that as early as possible in the lifetime of your events, you should focus on branding. This means that all event staff, including yourself, should wear company-branded clothing. The clothing that you choose should be appropriate for the type of event you have.

The more people are bombarded with your logo and your business name, and your event name, the more likely they will remember all those things and come back to attend future events.

So as you hire help and additional staff for your events, give them branded and appropriate clothing (in most cases at least t-shirts) to wear at the events.

Let me tell you about a revelation I once had when I was running my own events. It was a hike event, and I was walking and chatting with one of the hikers. The conversation turned to my own events and my website. Now mind you that I had gotten the URL for my website to be so simple that people could never confuse it or misspell it or forget it. The URL is comehike.com which is two very simple English words that make sense together and are almost impossible to misspell. That's what I thought anyway. That assumption quickly dissipated after the hiker with whom I was chatting said something like "what was your website name? Is it GoHike.com or GoHiking.com or LetsHike?"

This is when I realized that I can't rely on people to remember my business or website name no matter how simple or memorable the business name might seem to me.

What does that mean for you? You need to focus on your branding so that your attendees see your business name and website name many times throughout the event, and get used to it. Each extra time they see your business name, event brand, or website URL, it will increase the likelihood of them being able to remember it, re-connect online, attend more of your events, build more of a relationship with your business and event series, and hopefully eventually buy whatever you try to sell.

For that reason, having branded uniforms is extra important. So I would urge you to give it some priority. Plus, even though I don't run the hiking events anymore, I still have some of the t-shirts from those events that I sometimes wear, and it is nice to have them because they bring back all the fun memories I had running those events.

Plus, having branded uniforms will help the attendees know who the staff is and who can help them if they are confused with anything.

Now let's talk about how to hire the actual individuals after you find them online and after you have the uniforms for them. No matter how good their online reviews might be or what nice things they say about themselves, you should always meet them before the event. You don't need to meet them for a long time. Often, just a 10-15 minute conversation can help you understand whether they are appropriate for your event. You won't always be correct in that judgement that you get to form within 10-15 minutes, but you will certainly be able to weed out some of the very low quality people.

And that is what you really want to do: avoid hiring the bottom 25%. Hiring bad staff can turn your attendees off from your events, waste a lot of your time, some of your money, and discourage your other employees and lower overall morale. And if you can't have a person to person meeting with potential hires, at least take the time to talk to them on the phone to see how they communicate, how pleasant they might be, and get a feel for other things that they do or do not bring to the table.

Once you do add staff members, make sure that you welcome them and make them feel like an important part of the team by giving them specific responsibilities. Whenever people know what their jobs are, and what is expected of them, they make sure to do that. Even if they turn out to be slackers, most of the time they will still do the bare minimum main responsibility that you give them.

Overall, for all your staff, do try to make them feel like each of their unique tasks is very important and that they have a lot of responsibility. Make them feel respected, and keep an open door policy for them to be able to reach out to you and talk to you about anything at almost any time. Sometimes they won't like the job, but out of appreciation and respect for you, they will be motivated to do it better. And take the time to greet all your staff and thank them for their unique contributions. They will appreciate it.

Pro tip: when you thank anyone, don't just give them a plain thank you. It is really impersonal, and simply saying "thank you" that you easily give just about everyone else doesn't show a whole lot of appreciation. After all, how much effort did it take you to quickly say thanks and forget the person?

Instead of giving a simple thanks, tell them thank you for whatever good thing they did. For example, "thank you for managing attendance so carefully" or "thank you for being so proactive to help people find their seats" or other similar ways to express your gratitude. Thanking for specific things gets much more appreciation from whoever you are thanking.

6. Do you need to register your event as a business entity?

This is a legal discussion. And I am not a lawyer. So I must add the disclaimer that for true legal advice you should contact a lawyer or at least some legal professional who can be more authoritative and credible on the subject.

Full disclaimer: I do not give any legal advice anywhere in this book.

Disclaimer two: The issues I will discuss here apply to United States law only. If you are in a different country, please research what laws apply to your unique situation wherever you are located.

I did make a full online course on small business law with my lawyer. You can check out how to get it for free at the very end of the book where I discuss the free gifts I offer to readers of this book, and some of the very affordable additional resources and help.

But let's return to the main subject matter of this book. Here I'll just give you a few basic things to keep in mind when it comes to understanding whether you need to register your events as a business, or run the events "as self" which is what happens when you don't have a business entity.

One of the biggest benefits of registering a business entity and running your events under that business entity is that you get limited liability protection. That means that if someone sues you, and wins, they don't sue you for your personal assets like your money, house, car, furniture or clothing. All they do is sue the business. But if you don't open a company and don't run your events under that company, if someone sues you and wins, they will be suing you for your actual personal possessions and the money in your bank account, your car, your house and so on. You can potentially stand to lose everything you personally own.

So registering a business and running your events under that business can help you decrease the risk of losing your and your family's house, possessions and savings.

In United States, you register a business by going through your state's Secretary Of State Office. Every state has a Secretary Of State Office, and you can contact your state's office online or on the phone, and they will explain to you the steps you need to go through in order to register your business entity.

There is also some consideration of what kind of a business entity to open. It will also have tax implications. But since I am neither an accountant or a lawyer, and not truly qualified to advise on those issues, I will defer you to get help from those professionals on these issues. I would also encourage you to explore the online business law course which I mentioned that I made with my lawyer. In that course he explains how you can decide what kind of a business entity is right for you.

7. Do you need to get insurance for your event?

The reasoning of whether to buy insurance for your event series is somewhat similar to the reasoning for whether you should register a business entity to get limited liability protection. It also depends on the kind of events you run.

If your events are something where people have a higher chance of having accidents or getting injured, then it begins to make more sense to buy insurance for your events. Similarly, if your events become very large, and people start seeing you as a bag of money, they might be more likely to make some claim of damages for one reason or another. And having insurance gives you a little more peace of mind.

But at the end of the day, insurance isn't free. It is a cost. And you must evaluate it as any other cost that you might incur in your business, and decide whether it is worth getting insurance for your business.

8. Getting an event venue

In this section of the book, I'll explain how to find a free or cheap event venue for your event series.

Having a venue means an increased cost for your business. The cost isn't just financial. The cost is also your time and effort in doing appropriate research and due diligence, contacting different venues, talking to the managers there, scheduling (and rescheduling) things, and many more organizational details, all of which take up your time which significantly adds to the overall expense of getting a venue.

Since actual venues have a financial cost to them, at first consider what free options you have. The most common free option to run your events outside. While this is obviously not a possibility for all types of events, it works great for exercise groups. If the weather is nice, it can work well for some hobby or interest groups. In fact, doing an event outside can give you extra marketing because random people outside might see your big and fun gathering and might inquire about your events, and eventually might become attendees themselves.

Even if the kinds of events you put on don't immediately seem like they can be put on outside, give it some thought. You might come up with some creative and even fun solution that could make it more enjoyable for your attendees, save you money on not needing a venue, and might even give you a unique marketing angle if you do figure out something creative for how you will run your event outside.

The second option you have to get a free venue is to put on your events in coffee shops, restaurants or bars. Those kinds of venues really like it when you bring them people during off-peak hours. During peak hours they are usually overfilled, but in off-peak hours they are often empty. And if you can bring 10-20 (or however many) people to their businesses during off-peak hours, they might offer some extra group discounts, and welcome the potential customers that you will bring them.

The problem with coffee shops, restaurants or bars is that usually most events happen during weekends or evenings, which is their peak hours because that is when most people are off from work. So it isn't actually easy to bring them many people in non-peak hours, and it still leaves the problem of finding a venue for peak hours.

The next strategy to get a free venue is to find companies that have office spaces. These companies should target the same types of people that your events tend to attract. This way, if the events are in the evenings or weekends, most of the company staff is out of the office, and the meeting rooms become available. They often welcome events there because it means extra awareness and promotion to those businesses to your attendees, some of whom might get interested in the products and services of that business.

So you must network and reach out to managers at companies which target the same sort of customers as your event series draws, and you might work out a deal to get free space to run your events in exchange for a little bit of extra promotion for that business.

At some point, when you generate significant demand for your events, you will outgrow these types of mid-side event spaces. Congratulations if you are at that point!

If you begin to need bigger spaces, you can rent space in hotels. They often have "ballrooms" which they rent out to different events. And once you outgrow that, you can rent out full events spaces.

But generally, over 90% of the kinds of events that might be run by individuals or small businesses never need hotel ballrooms or large event or conference spaces. So if you are resourceful and creative, you should be able to get free (or extremely discounted) event spaces as your events grow.

9. Prizes and raffles to make your event more fun and attractive

Some event organizers like to give away prizes or raffles at their events. It makes the events more fun, memorable, and adventurous for your attendees.

The challenge with giving things away is that you are losing money by giving things away. So ideally, you would give things away from sponsors whom you can promote while announcing the raffle and then again when announcing the winner of the raffle.

Sponsors do tend to take a long time to get on board. So if you want to have raffles and prizes at your events, you must do two things:

1) Get on their radar early and start a conversation with them about potentially sponsoring the events. It will take time for their internal company discussions and any business development matter to get resolved. So the sooner you start pursuing this, the sooner it will happen for you. Don't only focus on this in the last minute.

2) Don't try to get sponsors too early. Sponsors want to reach many highly targeted people. So if you don't have too great of an attendance at your events just yet, first focus on growing your event series, and once you have the people, the sponsors will come.

10. Summing up the first chapter

Now you have a solid grasp of event fundamentals. What's left? Of course, the important thing that is left is promoting your events and growing attendance. The entire next chapter will focus on this.

In the next chapter I will explain what it took for me to find significant growth and attendance for my events, and how you can do the same (or hopefully much better!).

And one housekeeping note:

What do you think of this book so far? If you like it, it would be amazing if you could add a review about it on Amazon. And if you think the book can be improved, I am always looking for ways to improve the book so please email me with suggestions for how to improve it at:
alex.genadinik@gmail.com

Now please enjoy the second part of the book, on how to market and grow your event series.

CHAPTER 2: EVENT MARKETING AND GENERATING AMAZING ATTENDANCE

"Do what you can, with what you have, where you are."
- Theodore Roosevelt

Let's explore what's to come in this marketing section. I will explain to you how to use scalable online marketing strategies, leverage SEO (search engine optimization), your website and other online websites to draw people to your events, and then to make your attendees long-term attendees and clients of your other products and services. I will also explain how to get your events to really stand out, and generate publicity and extra attention.

These strategies worked like a charm for me. But it does take attention to detail from you, and a serious effort from you. So please follow the suggestions carefully.

Additionally, some of the topics like SEO are pretty gigantic topics to cover in enough detail in this book, the focus of which is events and not SEO. For topics like that, at the end of the book I will have a way for you to get free and affordable online courses on topics like SEO and many more additional resources, or my one-on-one coaching to help you create a really good marketing strategy for your event series.

1. Collecting contact information and building regular attendance

Do you ever hear people mention how email marketing is gold, and that this is where they truly make their money? Do you wonder how or why it is specifically email marketing?

I will tell you. The secret is in the fact that people almost never change email addresses, and it is a relatively intimate place to reach them. If people open your emails, chances are that they will read your email. And if your emails regularly bring them great value, interest or entertainment, they will engage with your mailings more and more.

Precisely this intimate re-engagement and your ability to reach people time and time again is why email marketing can be so much more effective than other promotional methods at generating clients and increasing engagement.

This section goes a little bit beyond email in suggesting that you collect any kind of contact information in an effort to be able to broadcast future announcements to your audience as much as possible.

In addition to collecting email addresses, try to get people to follow you on Twitter, or like your page or group on Facebook or connect with you on LinkedIn. The goal isn't for you to get more likes. The goal is to be able to re-engage those people in the future in as many ways as possible in the future when you need to promote new events or anything else to them.

What is the common thread here? In all these cases you will have a way to reach those people when you announce your upcoming events **and** all those platforms also make it relatively easy to get those people to forward the information about your events to their friends, and invite their friends to come to your events.

Of all those social platforms, on average, getting people's email addresses and marketing future events to them via email is by far much more effective than Twitter, Facebook or other social sites. So while the most coveted piece of contact information to collect is an email address, redundancy in having multiple points of contact is most ideal. So if you can, get people's email addresses AND Twitter AND get them to engage on Facebook, LinkedIn or wherever else your event series has a presence. It becomes that much more effective since on average they will get more reminders about your future events.

Ideally you want to build long-term fans. The more people will attend your events, the more they will spend directly on attendance fees, and the more likely they will be to engage with any other products or services that you try to sell them in the future. So having a way to remind them of upcoming events or any other future promotions is crucial.

For any business, a large part of the marketing focus should be on retaining existing customers because as a rule of thumb, it is easier to sell to an existing customer than to sell to a new customer. And since existing customers already trust you more, they may also spend higher amounts of money.

Here are the ideal times when to try collecting email addresses and contact information:

- When people sign up for your events online
- When people register at the event as they arrive to the place of the event
- When you run raffles and prize giveaways, collect business cards
- Always remind people to follow you on Twitter and like your page or join your group on Facebook. You will be able to promote your future events there to them.
- During the event, if possible, have a highly visible spot where you keep the URLs to your Twitter or Facebook pages, and your website.
- During the event, take a moment to remind your attendees to follow, like, or subscribe to your email newsletter to get notified when you schedule upcoming events.

And most importantly, one of the biggest factors in helping you get repeat attendance is the event quality itself. Do what you can to put on events that are as best as reasonably possible. The more people like your events, the more they will naturally come back, and your email reminders will be a welcome thing to them.

The big point to ponder and focus on: everything you do should have a focus to retain your customers long-term and get regular attendees for multiple events. This is why I emphasized this point as the very first thing I wanted to cover in the marketing section. If you can get someone to attend many of your events and engage in additional things you sell, you can earn thousands of percent more revenue from them compared to what they would spend if they only attended one of your events.

2. Attracting attendance

Let me tell you how attendance grew at my own events. At first, almost no one attended outdoor events or hikes that I organized. I would get very few sign-ups on my website, come to the event meeting point and have zero or one or two people join, and we would go on a hike together. I still had to put on a happy face, but inside I was very sad and disappointed because my events were struggling, and I wasn't solving the poor attendance issue.

As an event organizer, having no attendance is just about the worst and most frustrating thing that can happen to you, and in the beginning, this is exactly what was happening to me. It was giving me a very dejected and empty feeling, and I was very discouraged about my entire business and event idea, and often thought about stopping the whole thing, calling it a failure, and moving on with my life.

Then one day I got advice from a very experienced business person whom I had the luck to meet at a networking event. I only had 2 minutes of conversation with him, but he advised me to try to get a lot of publicity and attention by doing some very risky or even illegal outdoor events or hikes.

At first, that advice was very disappointing to me. I didn't want to do anything illegal, nor did I know how to create such an event. But I started to give this sort of a concept some thought. And a few weeks later an idea hit me which would eventually pave the way to my success.

Let me tell you about this idea. At that time I was living in San Francisco, California. If you are not familiar with the geography of San Francisco, it is almost an island, and surrounded by water on three sides. There is a large and rocky coastline. And I learned that decades ago, before ships had good navigation systems, many ships would crash on the rocky coastline and sink. I also learned that during low tide, some of those shipwrecks were visible.

That was my AHA! moment. I was going to organize a hike during low tide to catch a glimpse of the shipwrecks! I was very excited (partially because I am such a nerd, and myself wanted to see the shipwrecks more than anyone). I posted this event on my website, and a couple of other websites, and waited for an increased number of attendees.

I waited and waited...and waited, and people still weren't signing up on my website. So I thought that it was going to be another dud event. But like always, despite already preparing myself for disappointment, I came to the event meeting place about 15 minutes early as the punctual event organizer that I am.

But something was different about it this time.

Right where I planned my own event, stood a group of about 50 people who I didn't know. I thought "wow, that's just great. Not only will I have almost no attendees, but the few attendees that will come to my event will get confused by this large group of people." I was double disappointed and frustrated.

But then a funny thing happened. I asked those people what they were waiting there for, and they said they were there for a shipwreck hike that someone by the name of Alex Genadinik (that is me!!) organized.

I was floored! 50 people who came 15 minutes before the event! How? Why? What happened? These were all questions that raced through my mind.

I didn't have time to look for an answer to these questions because someone quickly pointed out to me that there was another group of about 40-50 people standing half a block away.

In a very confused, anxious, but excited. In that state I walked over to that group and asked them why they were there, and they too, told me that they were there for my event.

I invited them to join the original group, and as things got closer to the start time of the event people kept on rapidly arriving and swelling the numbers of my attendees. Many of them were bringing their kids to see the shipwrecks, their dogs and many friends.

People kept coming until about 15 minutes past when the event was supposed to start, and I had easily 200-300 people on my hands. People were still arriving, but the now hundreds of people in attendance pressured me to get started with the event so I did.

I had absolutely no idea how to handle this number of people. We were supposed to go on a hike, and walk on a trail that is at most 2-people wide. And there was only one of me. If I led the hike, how would I know what is happening at the end of the hike? If I walked in the middle of the group or in the back, the people in the front would have no idea where to go. In short, it was insane.

I completely mismanaged the hike, but I could not be more excited about the number of attendees that finally came to my event after all that effort and frustration. After regularly having less than 5 people join my hikes, this was such a happy relief.

You may be wondering how I got such large attendance all of a sudden. I'll tell you. Because the headline of my event was so exciting (it was: "Shipwreck hunt during low tide in San Francisco"), it turned out to easily be the most exciting event in the city that day. It was incredibly unique. So the Sunday paper for the entire city of San Francisco ended up publishing a **front-page ad** about my shipwreck hike.

The big impact: The event title was so attractive, flashy and grabbed so much immediate attention that it literally drew the curiosity of local press, and got me publicity.

So guess what I did? Every week after that, I ran a new very flashy themed event. I added a hike through a military base, seasonal nature hikes, even geeky hikes to the statue of Yoda (for Stars Wars fans), scavenger hikes, and wine tasting hikes. And, of course, my biggest draw was the shipwreck hike which I made into a recurring, monthly event.

Not all the hike themes were a hit, but most were! All those flashy, attention-grabbing themes got me quite a bit of publicity.

In the next sections I will explain to you how exactly I leveraged that publicity to grow the events and my overall business even more.

3. Local event websites

Let me explain to you how a lot of the publicity even had a chance to happen in the first place. You might be asking yourself how the local newspaper found out about my shipwreck hike in the first place.

I'll tell you how, and the beauty of it is that you can easily reproduce that I did.

In whatever city you live, there are many local-event websites. Even if you live in a tiny town, the big city nearby has many websites that focus on local events. For every city, those websites are different so I can't tell you which one will work in your city. But I can tell you how to find them.

To find such websites for the big city that is most relevant for where you run your events, just search google for something like "your event type in city name" which in my case was "hiking in San Francisco" or "outdoor events San Francisco" and you will get many results. Or you can even search something more basic like "events in city_name" where city_name is the name of your city, to find all the sites that list events for your local area.

Some of those search results will be from event-listing websites where you can add your events! Those kinds of sites are referred to as user generated content websites where the users (you) can post content (your events).

Go through the first 50 listings of the search results or so to make completely certain that you don't miss any such sites that might not immediately show up on the first page. In my case, I identified about 7 very good websites where I promoted every one of my events. It is on one of those websites that the local newspaper discovered my shipwreck hike, which resulted in all that extra publicity.

And the best thing is that if you post events there consistently (remember the idea of doing the events consistently that I mentioned in the beginning of the book?) the editors of those sites will begin to recognize your events, and give you extra promotion.

That is what happened in my case. Over time, I developed relationships with editors or owners of those event listing websites, and they gave me extra promotion every week because they knew that people loved my events and that I took the extra care and effort to make the events great and attractive.

This gave me a reliable weekly way to get great attendance to my events. And it was completely free. This is something you can easily reproduce on your own, wherever you might be located.

If you don't mind paying a few bucks, there are a couple of very affordable paid options which can give you an even bigger boost in attendance. I'll mention two such strategies here.

1) Meetup.com is a great website on which you can organize your own event group, and post your events. There are millions of people using Meetup.com worldwide and it is the single biggest events website in the world. It isn't free, but it is

very affordable. And if you can generate revenue from your events, the attendees that it will bring to your events will pay for the Meetup.com fees many times over. If I was starting a new event series today, it would be a an almost automatic choice for me to try to leverage meetup.com as best I possibly can. Meetup.com doesn't have to be (and shouldn't be) your only source for event promotion, but it is a great one to add to your list of promotion options.

Full disclaimer: I am **NOT** affiliated with meetup.com in any way

2) The other strategy you can try to use is the "promoted event" option that most local event websites offer. Usually the way these kinds of event listing websites work is they allow you to post your event listings for free. But if you pay them some fee like $19.99 or $29.99 or whatever they may charge (usually pretty affordable), they can give you a boosted premium listing which is sure to draw many more attendees to your events. And again, if you have a way to make money from your events, the revenue that you will generate from doing this should pay for the promoted listing fee and then some.

4. Your website

In addition to posting your events on large local-event websites, you can also create your own website, and post your events there.

Many people struggle with creating their own websites because it often takes a long time, and is expensive if you have to hire someone to create the website for you.

But luckily, there is Wordpress which allows you to create a great website on your own, for just about free, in a relatively short time. Wordpress now powers about 20% of all websites online, and is an industry standard for many types of businesses.

To help you create your own website without having to hire anyone, I created two online courses that can fully guide you through the process:

1) How to find a great domain name for your business
2) How to create a Wordpress website in as little as 1 day (or just a few days)

Discounts and ways to get the courses for *free* can be found in the very end of this book in the section with further resources.

So now you will be able to easily create your own website in just a few days, and all of a sudden more marketing options open up to you. You can now publish the event announcements on your website, and your website can rank in Google search for searches like "event type in city_name." For example, the important searches in my case were "group hikes in San Francisco" or "outdoor groups in San Francisco."

On your website you can also give people the option to sign up for your email updates and to follow you on your social media accounts. And that will allow you to reach people when you announce your future events, and turn people into regular attendees.

5. SEO (search engine optimization) for your website

SEO is a huge topic, and again, since it is outside the scope of event planning and marketing, I have a full course on this that will make you an SEO expert and help you understand how to make your website and pages rank well in Google searches.

I apologize for constantly mentioning the courses, but they are truly helpful, and get you up and running very quickly. Plus, since this is an event management and marketing book, many of the subjects around which I mention my courses (like building a website or SEO) don't fit into the scope of this book. So the courses are a fantastic resource for you to use.

Now that I explained myself, and why I keep alluding to the courses, let me explain why SEO is so important and after that I'll do my best to cover the basics of SEO that are relevant for your event marketing.

Imagine if you walk up to a random person and tell them to sign up for anything or buy something. In most cases they would just ignore you because either your offer or the timing of your offer isn't right for them. But when people search for something in Google, the timing and what they are searching for is exactly right for them right there and then. So a website visitor from Google search is typically much more engaged than some random person who might find you elsewhere.

Now that you understand why SEO traffic from Google is so valuable, let me explain some of the points of how this pertains to our event marketing.

Even though SEO is very complex, and I do strongly urge you to go through my online course on it, I can significantly simplify it here for you by tying many other parts of the strategy together.

First, I want to quickly go over the two most important concepts in SEO:

1) Choosing the kinds of keywords that you want your website to rank for is crucial. If I have hiking events, and people somehow discover me through searching "running in San Francisco" they will just click away because my site isn't relevant for them. But if the website ranks in Google for the exactly correct keywords that are relevant for the actual content of your website, the traffic will really engage with your website.

2) After you choose the correct keywords to rank for, you must actually begin to rank for those keywords in Google searches. And while there are many factors that go into getting your website to rank highly in Google searches, the single biggest ranking factor is the relevance, quality, authority, and quantity of the links that point to your website from other sites on the web.

Consider the second point, and now let me explain how the strategy comes full circle.

Remember how earlier in this chapter I explained how to get publicity and how to post your events on all kinds of different local event websites? Well, guess what? All those publicity and event-listing mentions usually have a link pointing from their websites to yours!!! Yes that deserved 3 exclamation marks!

Pursuing the strategy of getting publicity and getting links from other sites will boost you in Google search rankings, and over time, you will be getting lots of traffic and attendance from Google search because due to all those links pointing to your website, your website will rank highly in Google searches and draw a significant amount of traffic! Isn't that amazing? This is what happened in my business, and this is precisely what fueled a very large part of the growth of that business and my overall event series.

Let me actually tell you what happened in my business. After my website got publicity many times and was featured and linked to by many other websites, it started being very authoritative in Google search, and achieved very high Google search rankings. After I saw that, I started adding many new web-pages to the website, with each page targeting some new relevant search term to rank for. And most of the pages were ranking quite well, and bringing me more and more traffic.

This was essentially the key to the success of that business. I was able to grow search traffic, event attendance and revenue from publicity, social media sharing from my attendees, and from getting new attendees who discovered my events via Google search. I grew that business until I started my current business which helps entrepreneurs.

Over time, I moved from San Francisco and there was no one to run the events business, and it slowly declined, and now the website is just a shell of its former self.

But if I had wanted to, I could have stayed with that nice and lucrative San Francisco outdoors events business.

But don't feel sorry for me. I now have a great business that I love, which allows me to help other entrepreneurs like yourself, and it is truly my passion to help other entrepreneurs who might be just starting out so that you don't make the same mistakes that I did, and have an easier time finding success with your business than I did.

6. Branding

I already touched on branding earlier in the book. Here, I want to add just a few points on it.

First of all, one of the biggest and most memorable parts of your brand is the quality of the actual events. If people have a great time, you will have a great and loved brand. But if people have a boring or unsatisfactory time, that is also how your brand will be remembered.

And since your brand is ultimately the overall impression people have of your business, every point of contact they make with your event series from learning about, to registering for the events, to attending, has to be as high quality as possible.

That's all I wanted to note about basic branding because truthfully, I am much more excited about the next section which explains how to put your branding on steroids!

7. Branding on steroids

What I call branding on steroids, others sometimes call becoming a celebrity in your business niche. At first, this might sound a little funny, but bare with me. I'll explain the reasoning behind this, and hopefully you will see the awesome power of this strategy.

When I say celebrity, I don't mean like Kim Kardashian or Justin Beiber. What I mean is a business celebrity or a known person within your business niche, a thought leader or a mover and shaker if you will.

Once you are perceived as a leader in your business niche, people will suddenly want to network with you, do you favors, and to generally associate with you. This will give you more marketing, more authority, more publicity, and more trust from your potential customers, which will result in more sales since people need to trust you before they buy from you.

So how do you actually become a celebrity? It is actually not that difficult. What you must do is create a big platform for yourself or create a big product. Let me explain what I mean.

Think of any business celebrity. How did they get to be very well known in their industry? They either wrote a very successful book, had a very big YouTube or podcast show, or built a big company, and are now known through that. And having your own big event series can give you that big platform to stand on, and be known by. And of course, having lots of publicity that you might generate through the methods I outlined above can further help to establish you as somewhat of a celebrity in your niche.

Once you make your event series a very big and prominent one, you will be automatically seen as somewhat of a celebrity in your business niche. I am not saying that it will make you the top person in your niche, but I am saying that you will certainly be in the top 10% of the more powerful people in your niche, and many additional benefits will come from that long-term.

8. Generating publicity and standing out above the crowd

I already discussed how you can generate publicity for your business, but there is one more point I want to emphasize. It is that you should always try to stand out.

For example, recall how no one wanted to go on regular hikes with me, but hundreds of people wanted to go on a cool and exciting sounding hike.

This is what you should try to do with your event series. Think of what creative angles you can take, or do something more flashy that will make your events more memorable, and stand out.

Recall the advice I got from the experienced business person about doing something illegal or dangerous. I am not saying that you should try to do something illegal or dangerous. But try to think of any legitimate and on-brand way to get your events to stand out. The idea for this didn't immediately come to me. It took me weeks of thinking about it. But if you mull it over long enough, it will come to you.

9. Event video, live-streaming, and YouTube promotion

Another natural and nifty way you can promote your events is if you videotape your events (if that is possible in your unique situation), and then put those videos on YouTube and *properly* promote those videos.

This way, for very little additional effort, you can begin to have a presence on YouTube, and get that massive website to drive traffic and awareness to your events.

You can also have the YouTube video transcribed, and turned into a blog post which you can then share on social media, and get to rank in Google search, which would bring you even more traffic.

10. Making your event landing page highly converting and attractive

First thing is first. Your event headline must scream awesomeness, be exciting and inspire people to attend.

As I mentioned earlier, simple hiking event titles weren't that inspiring. But when I added exciting themes to the titles, the hikes suddenly began drawing more attention and attendance.

You can also add an element of scarcity to your event by communicating that this is a one of a kind event and won't happen again for a long time. This is what I did with the shipwreck hikes by noting that those hikes were happening at rare low tides.

Here is an example of a headline I used:

"Shipwreck hunt hike during rare low tide"

Do you see how the "rare low tide" makes it seem that this sort of thing can't just happen every day, and is in a way special?

Another thing you can do is if your event has an authoritative or famous person presenting or participating, you can hype up their credentials in the title or name-drop.

Spend quite a bit of time on your title. When people see a great title, it must make them curious so that they click on it, and move on to reading the event's description. If the title doesn't inspire, they don't click on it, and don't proceed to learn more about your event, and simply don't attend. The title is the hook. It is the way to grab people's attention. So do exactly that with your event titles: grab people's attention.

Once people click on your event title, they land on your event promotion page, and see every other detail of your event, starting with the description of the event.

In the description of your event you must reinforce the uniqueness, credibility or scarcity themes you used in the event headline. You must also keep building excitement about the event by adding more details about how amazing it will be. Usually the excitement is built by explaining what the benefits to the attendee will be if they attend the event. Will they learn something new? Will they have an amazing experience? Will they meet new and interesting people? Make sure you convey your event's best benefits in your description, and get people truly picturing enjoying the benefits of event.

But before you get carried away with all that, make sure that you clearly state the day, time, price, location name and address, directions for how to get there, refund policy, and cases in which the event might be cancelled. That will make your event appear well organized. If your event is not well organized, people might get turned off and simply move on from your event page, and you will never know why they left. Do keep in mind that many people simply leave if the event seems poorly organized. So make sure that you have all your ducks in a row because they leave in silence and you simply have smaller attendance than you usually would have, without even knowing that this was the case since they never inform you that they might have come to your event but decided not to engage because it seemed poorly organized.

Make sure to also include the speaker's or organizer's picture and bio in the event description. That makes things more personable for potential attendees, and helps people have more of an understanding of what they will get out of the event. A great person headlining your event can be a real attendance magnet. So a part of your job as the event manager and marketer is to constantly be looking for amazing and authoritative people to headline your events.

Another important part of your event page is a beautiful and inspiring event image. A great image will make people imagine and picture already having or enjoying the benefits outlined in the event. Once people are daydreaming about how amazing your event might be, and see themselves enjoying its benefits, they are almost sold on attending. So use a beautiful and inspiring image. It can go a very long way towards convincing people to attend.

Note about the image: make sure you have the rights to use the image commercially. Many people skip over this detail, but every once in awhile people get sued for copyright infringement, and that's no fun. So be careful about understanding the usage rights for a given image you are using in your event description if the image isn't yours.

And if you are comfortable with making videos, you can make a quick video outlining the benefits of the event to reinforce what you are already trying to express in the description. A good video can help you increase your event page's conversion rate, especially with those people who don't like to read and gloss over the written description.

Lastly, you must have a big call to action button for people to go ahead and register for the event. It must be prominent and highly visible. You can even have two such buttons. One can appear above the fold on top of the page, and one can appear towards the middle or bottom.

11. Pre-event build up with email marketing

An event is typically scheduled weeks in advance to give you a chance to do all the proper marketing, and allow people to plan for the event and fit it into their schedules.

If you have an email list, the best first place to announce the event and any early bird discounts is to your email list. If you don't have an email list, I would strongly urge you to begin building a list. A great place to start building your email list is by asking your event attendees to sign up for your email list. You can ask them to join your email list on your website and in person during event registration. This way your email list gets bigger with every event you put on, and your marketing becomes more powerful.

Whether you have your own email list or not, you should also ask any other people who are putting on the event with you to send an announcement to their email list. An example of who these people might be is a guest speaker or any partners, sponsors or collaborating organizations who are helping you put on the event.

When you send out the emails, they must have a great subject line and great content inside them that inspires people to attend.

The email headline is extremely important because it will play a large role in whether people open the email or just delete it. Your title must invoke some kind of an emotional response from people like interest or curiosity.

When you do send your emails, try to have a pre-event promotion schedule where you send an event promotion email on a Sunday and on a weekday that is preferably on of either Monday, Tuesday or Wednesday because those are the highest web traffic days for most businesses. This way you will be able to hit people who are more engaged on the weekends and those who are more engaged on the weekdays.

One thing you can also do is use social proof. If you have positive feedback from previous events or credentials for the speakers or event participants, use them as a quotes in your emails.

If the event is paid, you can create an email promotion schedule that coincides with your discount schedule. For example, you can have an early bird discount deadline, another smaller discount deadline, and another reminder for people to sign up before the prices actually go up. This creates urgency in people's minds and also gives you an excuse to send more email reminders.

You can also send out another email when the attendance capacity is almost full, which will further increase the feeling of scarcity, and inspire people to register.

12. Pre-event build up with social media

Events are social and visual things, and that makes social media a natural place to promote them.

It is a good idea to at least have a Facebook group, Twitter account, and possibly an instagram account to share photos of the events and get buzz going. You also want to post on Google+ and LinkedIn.

One thing you want to do from the beginning is to also create a hashtag for your events. That will help you understand what your attendees are saying about the event, and get even more of a buzz going around your events. There will be more on this a little bit further in the book.

You also want to use social media to promote your discounts and let people know when those discounts are expiring to get people to take action.

And of course you also want to use social media to interact with the event speakers or other event organizers or sponsors to share each other's posts and cross-pollinate your followers to maximize your social media reach.

Generally be active and enthusiastic on social media. If you don't mind the lack of privacy, include your personal Facebook friends, and invite them to attend and share your events. Your personal contacts can be a great source of support and attendance.

Also make sure to post lots of great content from other thought leaders in your niche. They might see that, and share your posts which will get you in their good graces, and also get you some of their social media followers.

Many of your tweets and social posts can be scheduled far in advance, using tools like HootSuite or Buffer.

When you do post on social media, use beautiful and inspiring images that stand out. That will give your posts more attention which will turn into more engagement, comments and hopefully larger attendance.

13. Boosting attendance from the registration thank you page

Do you know when people are most excited about your event? They are most excited and enthused about it when they themselves register. So on the thank you page of the registration when people complete the registration process, suggest to them to invite their friends along, or to share the event on their social media accounts. That will get you a small boost in attendance from those invites.

Additionally, once people sign up for the event, they will also get a thank you email with the event registration confirmation. You can use that email to make another suggestion for people to either invite friends to attend, share the event on social media, or to follow you on social media.

14. Promotion of the event during the event

During the event, you have an opportunity to raise buzz about it. Make sure to live tweet about the event, and encourage your attendees to also live tweet during an event. You may even run some kind of a small contest with people voting right on Twitter. That will get many people to tweet about your event, and inadvertently promote your event to their followers, many of whom may have similar interests as your attendees, and may be likely to become interested in the event after seeing it on Twitter.

You can also listen for quotable content that might occur during the event, and post it on Twitter as the event is happening. For example, if someone says something interesting during the event, tweet it out and mention that person in the tweet. Whenever they check their Twitter account next time they will see that you quoted and mentioned them, and possibly retweet it.

Try to also take photos of the event and share it on social media during the event. If any of the attendees check the Twitter hashtag stream of the event, and see themselves in the pictures, they might retweet it.

Additionally, if you hold some kind of a contest or a raffle during the event, it can be a good time to highlight a sponsor by giving away something of theirs while at the same time collecting email addresses of your attendees. Having those email addresses will allow you to remind them of future events and generate increased attendance by having more repeat attendees.

15. Promotion of the event after the event

Follow up the event with a blog post about the event and include any photos or videos you may have taken. When you send out this blog post to your email subscribers or social media followers, the people who didn't attend might have their mind changed for next time, and the people who did attend will get a reminder of how great it was, and will be encouraged to attend again. Plus, if the people who attended the event see themselves in the photos or event videos, they might share that on their social media, giving you a little bit of extra promotion.

You should also say thank you to your attendees in a post-event email. In this email you can ask for feedback on how you can improve the event moving forward, and encourage your attendees to also follow you on other social networks. The more places they follow you the less likely they will be to miss your future announcements about upcoming events.

By now you are probably able to guess what I'll suggest you do on social media after the event, right? Make sure to share the blog post, photos and any videos on your social networks.

Keep sharing until you will need to promote another future event, at which time you will start the whole event marketing cycle all over again, with the main difference that by then you will have many more social media followers and email subscribers, and a more engaged existing base of people to promote your future events to.

And that should grow with every event you put on, which should set you up for amazing growth.

CHAPTER 3: EVENT MANAGEMENT CHECKLIST

i. Set the goals and objectives for your event series or single event

Do you want the event to make money as your main income? Or do you want the event to funnel customers to a business of yours? Do you want the event to be more social than anything else?

It is easy to say yes to all of the above in almost all cases, but you must identify your most important goal. That will help you focus all your planning and strategy around achieving that goal.

ii. Put together a team

For many events, and especially when you are first starting out, you may be able to put on the event on your own.

But if you have 30-50 or more people attending an event, it usually helps if you have additional people on your staff to help you answer questions, help with organization of the event, and to bring additional skills to the event like video recording, photography, or something else that may be valuable for your event.

Additional types of team members may be your event co-organizers, basic staff to help with organization tasks like checking people in and making sure they are seated, and know where to go. You can also have staff that helps you with social media or publicity or other marketing.

Even during my hiking events which had no venue, no presenters or speakers and no recording, I could have really used additional staff. For example, if I was leading a hike and was in front of the group, that meant that there was no one to help the lagging people if they got lost or injured or anything else happened that required my attention. So even for simple events, additional staff is still very helpful.

iii. Set a date for the event

This point is obvious, but just make sure you have a clearly defined event date that is on a date that doesn't have other competing world events like the Super Bowl or Christmas or anything else that will compete with your event for attention and attendance.

iv. Create an event name and figure out your branding

The name of the events can be the same as your company name or something similar to it. The idea behind branding is to help people recall and recognize your events and your business because even though the event seems memorable to you, people are busy and have many things that distract them. That makes them likely to forget your event and your company name. But if the logo, catchy and unique event slogan, event name or the name of your company pop up and repeat somewhere in the future, having consistent branding will help people recall your events more readily. Sometimes that makes the difference between retaining an attendee and not.

v. Venue

Most events need to be held somewhere. In my case I ran hikes in parks and didn't need to book an event space, but most events do need to have reserved spaces that can accommodate all the attendees.

You must either find a way to secure free event space or find a way to have enough of a budget to pay to rent a venue. In many cases, the venue can be the most expensive part of hosting the event so this is a big challenge to overcome.

You must also make sure that people can easily get to the venue, and make their way in without too much backup, and be comfortably seated once they do get there.

Having some organization donate their space to your event for the duration of the event is a great way to get your first sponsor.

vi. Speakers, presenters and activities

You must make sure to secure the services of the speakers, educators, guides or entertainers who will be the main attractions of the events.

vii. Additional logistics and budget

You have to make sure all the details of the event are taken care of. Attention to detail is what sets your events apart in quality, and make them seem professionally put together.

These are things like smoothly handling registration, making sure that the attendees clearly understand the event itinerary and what to expect from the event.

You must also identify your budget because that will inform your decision of how much you can spend on event staff, event logistics and the venue itself.

viii. Identify, contact and form relationships with partners and sponsors

Whenever possible it is great to have promotional partners or promotional or financial sponsors. Try to have a strategy for how you will secure such partners or sponsors.

iv. Marketing plan

This book spent a lot of time on marketing because the marketing for your event is incredibly important because that is how you will get your attendees. So make sure that you have a solid plan for how you will get attendance because your ability to generate attendance and get attendees for your events will be the lifeline of your entire event series.

v. Evaluation process to determine whether the event was successful

How do you know if your event is successful? In my case, I was ecstatic when my event attendance started to grow significantly, and felt that this made it successful. But that was just the beginning because what about generating event revenue? Event after you generate revenue and make a profit, that is not the end of it either because what you also need is to have repeat attendance which means that you have to be very concerned about event quality.

Whatever your goal is, make sure that you can objectively identify and evaluate whether the event was a success on all measures. And if the event isn't a success on all measures, then you have some problem solving to do to figure out how to improve those aspects of your events which didn't go as great as you wanted.

vi. Evaluation process to determine whether the event was successful FOR YOUR ATTENDEES

Try to have some sort of a feedback loop. It can be as simple as talking to people during the event, and getting their feedback about it. You can also ask for feedback in an anonymous survey that you send out after the event. Doing this will give you direct hints at what you can improve for your next events, and improve your event series every time.

THE END

MORE OF MY BOOKS THAT CAN HELP YOU

1) Business Plan Template - (top business planning book on Amazon) every business should have a strong business plan. Don't start your business unitl you have a good business plan and a solid strategy to have your business succeed.

https://www.amazon.com/Business-plan-template-example-business/dp/1519741782

Shortened URL if you are using a print copy of this book:

https://goo.gl/rVoYe6

2) 10 Fundraising Strategies - almost all entrepreneurs ask about raising money, and you may be wondering about it too. This book gives you 10+ different strategies to raise money for your business.

https://www.amazon.com/10-Fundraising-Ideas-Strategies-strategies-ebook/dp/B00KADT0Q2

Shortened URL if you are using a print copy of this book:

https://goo.gl/3fqmBr

3) 20 Productivity Principles - this book will help you get more done regardless of what you are working on. I put together 20 different fields of productivity, each of

which can give you the strategies to align your work in order to get more done starting today and every day for the rest of your life.

https://www.amazon.com/Principles-Productivity-Motivation-Organization-Procrastination-ebook/dp/B06X96T4FZ

Shortened URL if you are using a print copy of this book:

https://goo.gl/m6PZQ1

Here is a full list of my 20+ books on Amazon:

https://www.amazon.com/Alex-Genadinik/e/B00I114WEU

Shortened URL if you are using a print copy of this book:

https://goo.gl/WWBcao

Note: if you are in the UK, change the .com in the URLs to .co.uk

FURTHER FREE RESOURCES

FREE GIFTS FOR YOU AND EXTRA RESOURCES

Gift 1: I will give you one free online business/marketing course of YOUR choosing and huge discounts on any additional courses.

I teach over 100 online courses on business and marketing. Just for you, I will give you one for absolutely free, and you get to choose which one. Browse my full list of courses and email me telling me which course you want, and I will send you a free coupon!

Here is my full list of courses:

https://www.udemy.com/user/alexgenadinik/

Send me an email to my personal emai at:
alex.genadinik@gmail.com

And tell me that you got this book, which of my courses you would like for free, and I will send you a coupon code to get that course for free.

Gift: 2: Get my Android business apps for free.

My apps come as a free 4-app course and iPhone and Android.

Free business plan app:
https://play.google.com/store/apps/details?id=com.proble mio&hl=en

Free marketing app:
https://play.google.com/store/apps/details?id=com.marke ting&hl=en

Free app on fundraising and making money:
https://play.google.com/store/apps/details?id=make.mon ey&hl=en

Free business idea app:
https://play.google.com/store/apps/details?id=business.id eas&hl=en

Here are my free apps for the iPhone:

Free business plan app:
https://itunes.apple.com/us/app/business-plan-and-coach /id554845193

Free marketing app:
https://itunes.apple.com/us/app/marketing-advertising-art icles/id587238156?ls=1&mt=8

Free app on fundraising and making money:

https://itunes.apple.com/us/app/funding-fundraising-ideas/id624657810?ls=1&mt=8

Free business idea app:
https://itunes.apple.com/us/app/small-business-ideas-help/id583498069?ls=1&mt=8

Gift 3: **Free business advice**

If you have questions about your events, your overall business, or anything mentioned in this book, email me at alex.genadinik@gmail.com and I will be happy to help you. Just please keep two things in mind:

1) Remind me that you got this book and that you are not just a random person on the Internet.
2) Please make the questions clear and short. I love to help, but I am often overwhelmed with work, and always short on the time that I have available.

COMPLETE LIST OF MY BOOKS

If you enjoyed this book, check out my Amazon author page to see the full list of my books:

http://www.amazon.com/Alex-Genadinik/e/B00I114WEU

And here is my website with all my work:

http://www.problemio.com

Thank you for reading and please keep in touch!

ABOUT THE AUTHOR

Alex Genadinik is a software engineer, successful entrepreneur, and a whiz marketer. Alex is a 3-time best selling Amazon author. His work has helped millions of entrepreneurs. You can learn more about Alex's current projects on his website: http://www.problemio.com

Alex has a B.S in Computer Science from San Jose State University.

Alex is also a prominent online teacher, and loves to help entrepreneurs achieve their dreams.

Here is a full list of books by Alex Genadinik on Amazon: http://www.amazon.com/Alex-Genadinik/e/B00I114WEU

Here is a shortened URL for the full list of books: https://goo.gl/uKk98y

Made in the USA
Lexington, KY
19 December 2017